AF452907

London Published by Richard Phillips, New Bridge Street

Vulgar Astonishment

Printed for Richard Phillips, New Bridge Str. 1807.

Doubt

Printed for Richard Phillips New Bridge Street 1807.

Sublime admiration.

Printed for Richard Phillips, No. 7 Bridge Street.

Prelude
Printed for Richard Phillips, New Bridge Street, Blackfriars.

Fashionable Impudence.

Printed for Richard Phillips, New Bridge St. 1807.

Rustic Cunning

Published by Richard Phillips, New Bridge Str. 1807.

Enthusiasm

Published for Richard Phillips, New Bridge Street

Expectation

Published by Richard Phillips, New Bridge Street.

L'Espoir

Astonishment

Printed for Richard Phillips, New Bridge Street.

Persuasion repulsed.

Supplication.

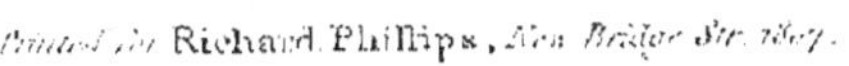

Printed for Richard Phillips, New Bridge Str. 1807.

A Discovery

Printed for Richard Phillips New Bridge St. 1807

Terror

Pub.d for Richard Phillips New Bridge St. 1807

False Gesture

Printed for Richard Phillips, New Bridge St.

Voluptuous Indolence.

Printed for Richard Phillips, New Bridge St. 1807.

Affection.

Published by Richard Phillips, Bridge Street, 1807

Voluptuary.
Printed for Richard Phillips New Bridge Street 1807.

Despondency —

Dejection

Sublime Adoration.

Printed for Richard Phillips New Bridge St. 1807.

Idiotism.

Printed for Richard Phillips, New Bridge Street.

Hearty Welcome

Published by Richard Phillips, New Bridge Street.

False Gustavus

Starting from repose.

Printed for Richard Phillips, New Bridge Street, 1807.

Apprehension

Printed for Richard Phillips, New Bridge Street

Obsequiousness.

Printed for Richard Phillips, New Bridge Str. 1807.

Printed for Richard Phillips New Bridge Street

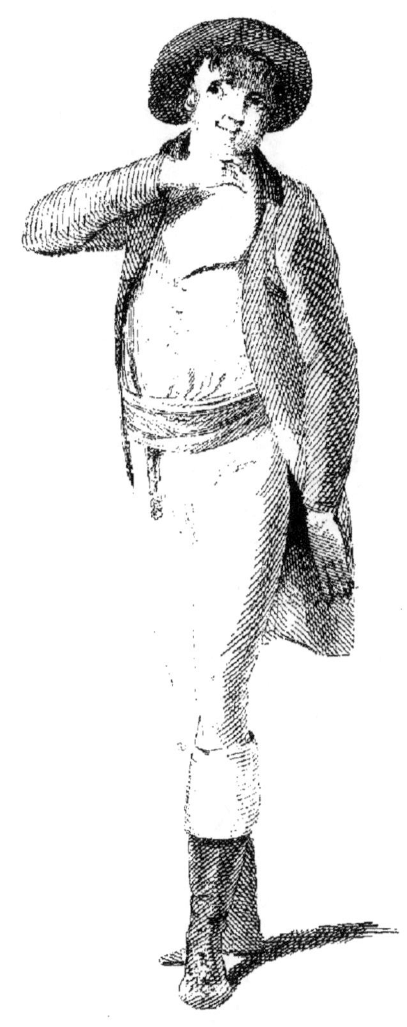

Contempt.

Printed for Richard Phillips, New Bridge St. 1807.

April.

Printed for Richard Phillips, New Bridge Street 1807.

Phlegm.

Printed for Richard Phillips, New Bridge Str. 1807.

Distraction & Persuasion

Printed for Richard Phillips New Bridge Street

Printed for Richard Phillips New Bridge Street.

Printed for Richard Phillips New Bridge Street

Reproach?

Printed for Richard Phillips. New Bridge Str. 1807.

Convict

Agility.

Printed by Richard Phillips, New Bridge Street.

Painful recollection
Pub. Oct. 1 by Richard Phillips New Bridge St.